The Economics of Inequality: A Call to Action for Politicians

Copyright Page

TITLE: The Economics of Inequality: A Call to Action for Politicians

1ST Edition

Copyright @ 2023

ISBN: 9798223939269

Table of Contents

The Economics of Inequality: A Call to Action for Politicians

By Roberto Miguel Rodriguez

Chapter 1: Introduction to Income Inequality

Understanding Income Inequality

In today's world, income inequality has become a pressing issue that demands the attention and action of politicians across the globe. This subchapter aims to provide a comprehensive understanding of income inequality and its various aspects, ranging from world income inequality to income inequality in specific sectors and regions.

World's Income Inequality:

The first step in addressing income inequality is to recognize its global scale. The world is facing an alarming wealth gap, with a significant portion of the population struggling to meet their basic needs while a small elite enjoys immense wealth. Understanding the causes and consequences of this disparity is crucial for policymakers to design effective strategies.

Gender Income Inequality:

Gender income inequality is a persistent problem that hampers social progress and economic growth. This section explores the reasons behind the wage gap between men and women, including discriminatory practices, occupational segregation, and the undervaluation of women's work. Policymakers must acknowledge and address these factors to create a fair and inclusive society.

Racial Income Inequality:

Racial income inequality continues to be a major challenge, perpetuating social and economic disparities. This portion delves into the historical and structural factors that contribute to this inequality, such as discrimination, unequal access to education, and biased employment practices. Politicians must actively work towards dismantling systemic barriers and promoting equal opportunities for all races and ethnicities.

Income Inequality in Education:

Education is often touted as the great equalizer, but income disparities significantly impact access to quality education. This section examines how economic inequality affects educational opportunities, leading to a cycle of intergenerational poverty. Policymakers must prioritize investments in education, particularly for underprivileged communities, to bridge this gap and pave the way for social mobility.

Income Inequality in Healthcare Access:

Access to healthcare should be a basic human right, but income inequality creates significant disparities in healthcare access. This part explores how lower-income individuals face challenges in affording quality healthcare, resulting in poorer health outcomes. Policymakers must strive for equitable healthcare systems, ensuring universal access to medical services and addressing socioeconomic barriers.

Income Inequality in Developing Countries:

Developing countries often bear the brunt of income inequality, with limited resources and unequal distribution of wealth. This section sheds light on the unique challenges faced by these nations and the potential solutions to uplift their populations. Policymakers need to prioritize inclusive growth, invest in social infrastructure, and foster economic opportunities to reduce income disparities.

Income Inequality in Developed Countries:

Even in developed nations, income inequality poses significant socio-economic challenges. This portion examines the consequences of income inequality in advanced economies, including social unrest, decreased social mobility, and political instability. Policymakers must implement progressive taxation, robust social safety nets, and policies that promote fair wealth distribution to address this issue.

Income Inequality in Urban and Rural Areas:

Income inequality manifests differently in urban and rural areas. This section explores the disparities between these regions, including access to resources, job opportunities, and public services. Policymakers should focus on balanced regional development, ensuring equitable distribution of resources and addressing the unique needs of both urban and rural communities.

Income Inequality in the Tech Industry:

The tech industry has witnessed a surge in wealth creation, but it has also contributed to income inequality. This part discusses the concentration of wealth in the hands of a few tech giants and the impact on workers' wages. Policymakers must regulate the industry, promote competition, and ensure that technological advancements benefit society as a whole.

Income Inequality in the Gig Economy:

The rise of the gig economy has brought new challenges in income inequality. This section explores the precarious nature of gig work, the lack of benefits and job security, and the implications for workers' income. Policymakers must adapt labor laws to protect gig workers, ensure fair compensation, and provide social safety nets.

Understanding income inequality is a crucial first step for politicians to address this global issue. By comprehending the nuances of income disparities in various sectors and regions, policymakers can develop effective strategies to promote inclusive growth, reduce poverty, and create a fairer society. It is imperative that politicians take action and implement policies that prioritize equity, social justice, and equal opportunities for all.

Impact of Income Inequality on Society

Income inequality is a pressing issue that affects societies worldwide and has far-reaching consequences across various aspects of life. This subchapter aims to shed light on the multiple dimensions of income inequality and its impact on society, urging politicians to take action towards creating a more equitable and just society.

World's Income Inequality:

The global income gap has widened over the past decades, exacerbating social disparities and hindering progress. High levels of income inequality can lead to social unrest, political instability, and hinder economic growth. It is crucial for politicians to address this issue on a global scale, promoting policies that aim to redistribute wealth and ensure equal opportunities for all.

Gender Income Inequality:

Women continue to face significant wage gaps compared to their male counterparts, even in developed countries. This inequality not only affects women's economic independence and financial security but also perpetuates gender disparities in various spheres of life. Policymakers must strive to close the gender pay gap through measures such as pay transparency, affordable childcare, and promoting gender equality in the workplace.

Racial Income Inequality:

Racial income disparities persist in many countries, with minority communities facing lower wages and limited access to economic opportunities. This inequality deepens social divisions, perpetuates systemic racism, and undermines social cohesion. Politicians must address racial income inequality by implementing policies that promote anti-discrimination laws, affirmative action, and equal access to education and employment.

Income Inequality in Education:

Income disparities have a profound impact on educational opportunities, creating a cycle of poverty and limited social mobility. Students from low-income backgrounds often face inadequate resources, lack of quality education, and limited access to higher education. Policymakers must prioritize reducing income inequality in education by investing in public schools, providing equal access to quality education, and bridging the digital divide.

Income Inequality in Healthcare Access:

Income inequality directly affects healthcare access, with lower-income individuals facing barriers to quality healthcare services. Health outcomes are often closely tied to socioeconomic status, resulting in disparities in life expectancy, disease prevalence, and healthcare outcomes. To address this, politicians must ensure universal access to healthcare, invest in public health infrastructure, and prioritize healthcare affordability for low-income individuals.

Income Inequality in Developing and Developed Countries:

Income inequality is not limited to developing countries but also prevalent in developed nations. In both contexts, politicians must implement progressive taxation policies, promote inclusive growth, invest in social safety nets, and prioritize poverty alleviation. By narrowing the income gap, societies can foster greater social cohesion, reduce crime rates, and promote sustainable economic growth.

Income Inequality in Urban and Rural Areas:

Income disparities are often intensified in urban areas, where high costs of living and limited job opportunities further marginalize low-income individuals. Similarly, rural areas face unique challenges such as limited access to quality education, healthcare, and employment opportunities. Policymakers must address these disparities by investing in urban and rural infrastructure, promoting job creation, and implementing policies that bridge the urban-rural divide.

Income Inequality in the Tech Industry and Gig Economy:

The rapid growth of the tech industry and gig economy has exacerbated income inequality, with a small portion of individuals reaping the benefits while many struggle to make ends meet. Policymakers must regulate these sectors, ensure fair wages, and protect workers' rights. Additionally, investing in digital literacy programs and vocational training can empower individuals to thrive in the evolving job market.

In conclusion, income inequality has profound consequences on society, affecting various aspects of life, including education, healthcare, and social cohesion. Policymakers must prioritize addressing income inequality by implementing policies that promote wealth redistribution, equal opportunities, and social justice. Through proactive measures and a commitment to creating a fairer society, politicians can contribute to the well-being and prosperity of their constituents.

The Importance of Addressing Income Inequality

Income inequality is a pressing issue that demands the immediate attention of politicians across the globe. As the world grapples with the ramifications of this growing divide, it is crucial for policymakers to understand the multifaceted nature of this problem and take decisive action to address its root causes. This subchapter aims to shed light on the various dimensions of income inequality, including its impact on different sectors and demographics, and underscores the urgency for politicians to prioritize this issue in their policy agendas.

World's Income Inequality: Income inequality is not limited to a single country or region. It is a global concern that hampers social cohesion, economic growth, and political stability. By acknowledging the interconnectedness of economies and societies, politicians can work towards implementing coordinated policies that promote equitable growth and reduce the gaps between the rich and the poor.

Gender, Racial, and Educational Income Inequality: Income disparities based on gender, race, and education exacerbate societal divisions and hinder progress towards equality. Politicians must confront these systemic biases by promoting inclusive policies that empower marginalized groups, ensure equal pay for equal work, and improve access to quality education, thus providing pathways for upward mobility and reducing income inequality across these dimensions.

Income Inequality in Healthcare and Developing Countries: Income inequality directly impacts access to healthcare, perpetuating a cycle of poverty and ill health. By investing in robust healthcare systems and providing affordable and accessible healthcare services, politicians can bridge this gap and ensure that no individual is left behind due to their socioeconomic status. In developing countries particularly, targeted policies that address income inequality can help alleviate poverty and unlock economic potential.

Income Inequality in Developed and Urban Areas: While income inequality is often associated with developing economies, it is also prevalent in developed and urban areas. Rising housing costs, limited job opportunities, and unequal access to public services contribute to this disparity. Policymakers must implement measures to promote affordable housing, create inclusive urban environments, and foster economic diversification to address income inequality in these regions.

Income Inequality in the Tech Industry and Gig Economy: The rapid growth of the tech industry and the rise of the gig economy have further exacerbated income inequality. Politicians must address the challenges posed by these emerging sectors by introducing regulations that protect workers' rights, ensure fair wages, and promote access to training and upskilling opportunities, thus fostering a more inclusive and equitable economy.

In conclusion, income inequality is a complex and pervasive issue that requires the immediate attention of politicians worldwide. By addressing income inequality in its various forms, policymakers can create a more equitable and prosperous society, where opportunities for social and economic advancement are available to all. The time for action is now, and politicians must rise to the challenge and make tangible strides towards reducing income inequality for the betterment of their constituents and the world at large.

Chapter 2: World's Income Inequality

Overview of Global Income Inequality

Income inequality has become a pressing issue that demands the attention of politicians worldwide. In this subchapter, we will provide an overview of the various facets of global income inequality, highlighting its impact on different segments of society. By understanding the complexities and consequences of income inequality, politicians can effectively address these issues and strive for a more equitable society.

World's Income Inequality:

Income inequality is not limited to a particular country or region; it is a global phenomenon. The gap between the rich and the poor has widened significantly in recent decades, exacerbating social and economic disparities across nations. This section will explore the key factors driving global income inequality and the implications it has on global development and stability.

Gender Income Inequality:

Gender income inequality remains a persistent problem, with women consistently earning less than their male counterparts for similar work. This subchapter will delve into the underlying causes of gender income disparity, such as occupational segregation and discriminatory practices, and propose policy interventions to bridge the gap.

Racial Income Inequality:

Racial income inequality is a grave concern that perpetuates social injustices and hinders economic growth. This section will shed light on the systemic barriers faced by racial and ethnic minorities, including discrimination in employment, education, and access to financial resources. It will also explore strategies to dismantle these barriers and create a more inclusive society.

Income Inequality in Education:

Unequal access to quality education perpetuates income inequality and limits social mobility. This subchapter will examine the disparities in educational opportunities across different socioeconomic backgrounds, highlighting the consequences for individuals and society as a whole. It will propose policy measures to bridge the education gap and ensure equal opportunities for all.

Income Inequality in Healthcare Access:

Access to healthcare is a fundamental right, yet income inequality often results in disparities in healthcare access. This section will analyze how income inequality affects individuals' ability to afford healthcare services and the subsequent impact on health outcomes. It will propose strategies to improve healthcare access for marginalized communities.

Income Inequality in Developing Countries:

Developing countries face unique challenges in addressing income inequality. This subchapter will explore the factors that contribute to income disparities in these nations, such as limited access to education, inadequate social safety nets, and unequal distribution of resources. It will provide insights into effective policy interventions for reducing income inequality in developing countries.

Income Inequality in Developed Countries:

Income inequality is not solely a problem of developing nations; developed countries also grapple with this issue. This section will examine the causes and consequences of income inequality in advanced economies, including the concentration of wealth, wage stagnation, and the erosion of the middle class. It will propose policies to foster inclusive growth and reduce income disparities.

Income Inequality in Urban and Rural Areas:

Income inequality manifests differently in urban and rural areas. This subchapter will explore the unique challenges faced by each setting, such as urban poverty, lack of affordable housing, and limited job opportunities in rural areas. It will highlight the need for targeted policies that address the specific needs of urban and rural communities.

Income Inequality in the Tech Industry:

The tech industry has been a driver of economic growth but has also contributed to income disparities. This section will examine the impact of technological advancements on income inequality, including automation, job displacement, and the concentration of wealth in tech hubs. It will propose strategies to ensure that the benefits of the tech industry are shared more equitably.

Income Inequality in the Gig Economy:

The rise of the gig economy has brought new challenges in terms of income inequality. This subchapter will explore the precarious nature of gig work, the lack of labor protections, and the widening income gap between gig workers and traditional employees. It will offer policy recommendations to address the unique issues faced by gig economy workers.

In conclusion, understanding the multifaceted nature of global income inequality is crucial for politicians seeking to address this pressing issue. By examining the various dimensions of income inequality and proposing effective policy interventions, politicians can play a pivotal role in creating a more just and equitable society.

Causes of Global Income Inequality

Income inequality is a pressing issue that affects various aspects of our society, from economic growth to social stability. In order to address this issue effectively, it is crucial for politicians to understand the underlying causes of global income inequality. This subchapter aims to shed light on the key factors that contribute to income disparities across different sectors, regions, and demographics.

One major cause of global income inequality is the unequal distribution of wealth and resources. In many developed and developing countries, a small portion of the population holds a significant share of the nation's wealth, while the majority struggle to make ends meet. This wealth concentration exacerbates income disparities and limits opportunities for upward mobility.

Gender income inequality is another critical factor in global income disparities. Women, on average, earn less than men for similar work and face barriers to career advancement. This disparity not only affects individual women but also impacts families, communities, and the overall economy. Addressing gender income inequality requires policies that promote equal pay, improved access to education and training, and greater representation of women in leadership positions.

Similarly, racial income inequality persists in many societies, with marginalized racial and ethnic groups experiencing lower wages and limited economic opportunities. Systemic discrimination and biases in hiring practices contribute to these disparities. Policymakers must prioritize efforts to promote diversity, combat discrimination, and create inclusive economic environments.

Income inequality in education and healthcare access further perpetuates global income disparities. Unequal access to quality education and healthcare limits opportunities for individuals to improve their economic prospects. Investing in public education, expanding access to affordable healthcare, and implementing social safety nets can help level the playing field and reduce income inequality.

Developing countries often experience higher income inequality due to various factors such as limited access to education, political instability, and lack of economic opportunities. Policymakers need to prioritize inclusive growth strategies, invest in human capital, and promote sustainable development to address income disparities in these regions.

In developed countries, income inequality is often linked to technological advancements and automation, which lead to job displacement and wage stagnation for certain sectors of the population. Policymakers must prioritize policies that ensure technological advancements benefit all segments of society and provide support and retraining programs for affected workers.

Income inequality in urban and rural areas is also a significant concern. Urban areas tend to offer more job opportunities and higher wages, while rural areas often struggle with limited economic activity and lower wages. Policies that promote rural development, invest in infrastructure, and provide rural communities with access to essential services can help bridge this gap.

Lastly, income inequality in specific industries, such as the tech industry and the gig economy, also contribute to global income disparities. These sectors often offer high-paying jobs to a select few, leaving many workers with low wages and precarious employment. Implementing fair labor practices, promoting worker rights, and encouraging innovation and entrepreneurship can help address income disparities in these industries.

In conclusion, global income inequality arises from a complex interplay of various factors, including wealth concentration, gender and racial discrimination, limited access to education and healthcare, economic disparities between developed and developing countries, urban-rural divides, and sector-specific income disparities. To address this issue effectively, politicians must take a multifaceted approach, implementing policies that promote equal opportunity, inclusive growth, and social justice. By understanding and addressing the causes of global income inequality, policymakers can pave the way for a more equitable and prosperous future for all.

Consequences of Global Income Inequality

Income inequality has become a pressing issue in today's global economy. As politicians, it is essential for us to understand the consequences of this phenomenon and take appropriate action to address it. In this subchapter, we will explore the far-reaching implications of global income inequality across various dimensions, including gender, race, education, healthcare access, geography, and specific industries.

Gender income inequality is a stark reality that persists in many societies. Women consistently earn less than men, resulting in not only financial disadvantages but also reduced opportunities for career advancement and economic independence. This gender pay gap hampers overall economic growth and perpetuates societal disparities.

Similarly, racial income inequality is a significant concern. Minorities often face discrimination in the labor market, leading to lower wages and limited access to quality education and healthcare. This inequality not only undermines social cohesion but also hinders economic progress by excluding talented individuals from contributing fully to the workforce.

Income inequality in education exacerbates disparities in social mobility. Children from low-income families often lack access to quality education, limiting their future prospects and perpetuating the cycle of poverty. This divide not only affects individuals and families but also hampers a country's overall productivity and competitiveness.

The consequences of income inequality in healthcare access are equally severe. The less privileged struggle to afford adequate healthcare, leading to higher mortality rates and reduced productivity. This inequality not only affects individuals' well-being but also burdens healthcare systems and increases societal costs.

Income inequality in urban and rural areas also has distinct ramifications. Urban areas often concentrate wealth, leading to inflated living costs and limited affordable housing options. In contrast, rural areas suffer from limited economic opportunities and inadequate infrastructure, perpetuating poverty and depriving communities of essential services.

Moreover, income inequality in specific industries like the tech industry and gig economy further widens the gap between the rich and the poor. High-paying tech jobs primarily benefit a select few, while those in the gig economy often struggle with low wages and lack of job security. These disparities contribute to overall social and economic instability.

In both developed and developing countries, income inequality poses substantial challenges. In developed nations, it undermines social cohesion and exacerbates political polarization. In developing countries, it hampers poverty reduction efforts and perpetuates social unrest.

As politicians, it is our responsibility to address these consequences and promote policies that reduce income inequality. By implementing progressive taxation, investing in quality education and healthcare, and fostering inclusive economic growth, we can create a fairer society that benefits everyone. It is crucial to prioritize equal opportunities, social mobility, and sustainable development to build a more equitable future for all.

Chapter 3: Gender Income Inequality

Gender Wage Gap: Causes and Effects

Introduction:

In recent years, the gender wage gap has emerged as a critical issue in discussions surrounding income inequality and social justice. This subchapter aims to shed light on the causes and effects of the gender wage gap, providing a comprehensive understanding of this pervasive problem. Addressed to politicians, this chapter will equip them with the knowledge needed to enact policies that promote gender equality and reduce income disparities within various niches, such as the world's income inequality, gender income inequality, racial income inequality, income inequality in education, healthcare access, developing and developed countries, urban and rural areas, the tech industry, and the gig economy.

Causes of the Gender Wage Gap:

1. Occupational Segregation: Historically, women have been concentrated in low-wage sectors and underrepresented in higher-paying fields, perpetuating the wage gap.

2. Discrimination and Bias: Deep-rooted gender biases in hiring, promotion, and pay decisions contribute significantly to the wage gap, as women often face unequal treatment.

3. Motherhood Penalty: The wage gap widens for women who become mothers, as they face reduced opportunities for career advancement and are often forced to take on part-time or lower-paying jobs to balance work and family responsibilities.

4. Negotiation and Confidence Gap: Women tend to negotiate less aggressively and have lower self-confidence in negotiating salaries, leading to lower wages compared to their male counterparts.

5. Unequal Access to Education and Training: Limited access to quality education and training opportunities for girls and women further exacerbates the wage gap.

Effects of the Gender Wage Gap:

1. Economic Inefficiency: The gender wage gap hampers economic growth by underutilizing women's skills and talents, leading to a loss in productivity.

2. Poverty and Financial Insecurity: Women, especially single mothers, are more likely to experience poverty and struggle to meet their basic needs due to lower wages.

3. Inequality in Retirement and Wealth Accumulation: Lower wages for women translate into reduced savings and retirement benefits, leaving them vulnerable to poverty in old age.

4. Gender Inequality and Social Discontent: Persistent wage disparities contribute to social unrest and perpetuate gender-based discrimination and inequality in society.

5. Impact on Families and Communities: The gender wage gap affects families' well-being, limiting their ability to invest in education, healthcare, and other essential needs.

Conclusion:

Understanding the causes and effects of the gender wage gap is crucial for policymakers to address this issue effectively. By implementing policies that promote equal pay, combat discrimination, provide access to quality education, and support work-life balance, politicians can contribute to achieving gender equality and reducing income disparities in various niches. It is imperative that politicians recognize the urgency of closing the gender wage gap, as it not only benefits women but also fosters a more inclusive and prosperous society for all.

Discrimination and Bias in the Workplace

In today's society, discrimination and bias continue to persist in workplaces around the world, contributing to the perpetuation of income inequality. This subchapter aims to shed light on the various forms of discrimination that exist, including those based on gender, race, education, healthcare access, and geographic location. By understanding the nature and consequences of workplace discrimination, politicians can take necessary action to address these issues and promote greater equality.

Gender income inequality remains a pervasive problem across the globe. Women, on average, earn less than their male counterparts for performing the same work. This discriminatory practice not only hampers economic growth but also deepens societal inequalities. To overcome this, politicians must support policies that ensure equal pay for equal work and promote workplace diversity and inclusion.

Similarly, racial income inequality is a pressing concern in many countries. People from racial minority groups face disadvantages in accessing quality education, healthcare, and employment opportunities, leading to a significant income gap. Policymakers must enact legislation to dismantle systemic barriers, foster equal opportunities, and combat racial biases in the workplace.

Income inequality in education further exacerbates disparities in society. Children from low-income families often lack access to quality education, which perpetuates the cycle of poverty. Politicians should prioritize investment in education, particularly in underserved communities, to bridge this gap and provide equal opportunities for all.

The issue of income inequality in healthcare access is closely intertwined with workplace discrimination. Marginalized individuals often face limited access to healthcare services, resulting in poorer health outcomes and reduced economic opportunities. Policymakers must work towards universal healthcare coverage and address the underlying social determinants of health to ensure equal access to healthcare for all citizens.

Income inequality is not limited to developing countries alone; developed nations also grapple with this issue. Policymakers must implement progressive tax systems, improve social safety nets, and invest in job creation to reduce income disparities and promote inclusive economic growth.

Furthermore, income inequality persists in both urban and rural areas, albeit with different dynamics. Urban areas tend to concentrate wealth and opportunities, leaving rural communities behind. Policymakers should focus on rural development, investing in infrastructure, education, and job creation to bridge the urban-rural divide and ensure equitable distribution of resources.

The tech industry and gig economy are not immune to income inequality either. Politicians must address issues such as precarious work, lack of benefits, and unfair labor practices to safeguard workers' rights and ensure a fair distribution of income within these sectors.

In conclusion, discrimination and bias in the workplace perpetuate income inequality across various dimensions. By recognizing and addressing these issues, politicians can play a vital role in creating a more inclusive and equitable society. It is imperative for policymakers to enact legislation, invest in education and healthcare, and promote equal opportunities to bridge the income gap and foster sustainable economic growth. Only through collective action can we achieve a more just and prosperous future for all.

Policies to Reduce Gender Income Inequality

Gender income inequality remains a pressing issue across the globe, requiring immediate attention from policymakers. In order to address this issue effectively, it is crucial to implement targeted policies that strive to eliminate disparities and promote equal opportunities for all. This subchapter aims to outline some key policies that can be employed to reduce gender income inequality, focusing on the unique challenges faced by women in various sectors and regions.

Firstly, it is essential to encourage equal pay for equal work. This can be achieved by implementing legislation that mandates pay transparency, making it easier for women to identify and challenge wage discrimination. Additionally, promoting pay equity through proactive measures such as salary audits and affirmative action can help bridge the gender pay gap.

Secondly, enhancing access to quality education and providing equal opportunities for women in all levels of education is crucial. Initiatives such as scholarships and targeted support programs can empower women to pursue higher education and enter fields traditionally dominated by men, thereby increasing their earning potential.

Furthermore, we must address the gender disparities in the healthcare sector. Policies should focus on improving access to affordable and comprehensive healthcare for all, including reproductive health services. Additionally, promoting gender sensitivity and eliminating biases within the healthcare system can ensure that women receive equitable treatment and support.

In both developing and developed countries, targeted policies are required to address the unique challenges faced by women in urban and rural areas. Urban areas often witness higher gender income inequalities due to concentrated economic activities and gender biases in the labor market. Policies should focus on providing affordable childcare services, flexible work arrangements, and affordable housing to support women in urban areas. In rural areas, initiatives such as providing access to credit, promoting entrepreneurship, and investing in infrastructure can empower women economically.

Moreover, addressing gender disparities in the tech industry and the gig economy is crucial. Policymakers should work closely with the private sector to promote gender diversity and inclusion, ensuring fair representation and equal opportunities for women. Furthermore, implementing regulations to protect gig economy workers and guarantee fair wages and benefits is essential.

To effectively combat gender income inequality, policymakers must recognize the intersectionality of gender with other forms of inequality, such as racial income inequality and income inequality in education and healthcare access. Policies should be designed to address these interconnected issues, ensuring an inclusive and equitable society for all.

In conclusion, reducing gender income inequality requires a comprehensive approach that encompasses various sectors and regions. By implementing targeted policies such as equal pay, improved access to education and healthcare, and addressing disparities in specific industries, policymakers can make significant strides towards creating a more equitable society for all.

Chapter 4: Racial Income Inequality

Historical Context of Racial Income Inequality

In order to address the pressing issue of racial income inequality, it is crucial for politicians to understand its historical context. Racial income inequality has deep roots that stretch back to centuries of systemic oppression and discrimination. This subchapter aims to shed light on the historical factors that have contributed to the existing disparities in income and wealth among different racial groups.

Throughout history, racial minorities have faced various forms of discrimination, such as slavery, colonization, and segregation. These oppressive systems have had long-lasting effects on the economic opportunities available to different racial groups. For instance, slavery in the United States not only deprived African Americans of their basic human rights but also denied them the opportunity to accumulate wealth and assets, which has had intergenerational consequences.

Even after slavery was abolished, discriminatory practices such as Jim Crow laws and redlining continued to limit economic opportunities for racial minorities. These practices perpetuated segregation and denied access to quality education, housing, and employment opportunities, further exacerbating income disparities.

In addition to these historical factors, the ongoing effects of racial discrimination can be seen in the labor market. Racial minorities often face hiring discrimination, wage gaps, and limited access to promotions and leadership positions. This perpetuates a cycle of low-income and limited upward mobility for many individuals and families.

Addressing racial income inequality requires a multifaceted approach that takes into account historical injustices and their contemporary consequences. It is crucial for politicians to implement policies that tackle both the immediate and long-term effects of discrimination. This includes investing in quality education in underserved communities, promoting equal employment opportunities, and implementing anti-discrimination measures in the labor market.

Furthermore, politicians must also strive to dismantle systemic barriers that perpetuate racial income inequality. This includes reforming criminal justice systems, promoting fair housing policies, and addressing disparities in healthcare access. By addressing these structural issues, policymakers can work towards creating a more equitable society where individuals of all racial backgrounds have equal opportunities to thrive.

In conclusion, understanding the historical context of racial income inequality is essential for politicians seeking to address this pressing issue. By acknowledging the systemic discrimination and oppression faced by racial minorities throughout history, policymakers can work towards implementing comprehensive solutions that promote economic justice and equality for all.

Systemic Racism and its Impact on Income

Introduction:

In the pursuit of a fair and just society, it is imperative for politicians to understand and address the underlying causes of income inequality. One of the most significant factors contributing to this pervasive issue is systemic racism. This subchapter aims to shed light on the impact of systemic racism on income, exploring its effects in various spheres, including world income inequality, gender income inequality, racial income inequality, education, healthcare access, developing and developed countries, urban and rural areas, the tech industry, and the gig economy.

Understanding Systemic Racism:

Systemic racism refers to the deeply ingrained discriminatory practices, policies, and structures that perpetuate racial inequality and disadvantage certain racial or ethnic groups. Its far-reaching consequences extend beyond social and political realms, significantly impacting income disparities.

World Income Inequality:

Systemic racism plays a substantial role in exacerbating income inequality on a global scale. Historical exploitation, colonialism, and ongoing discriminatory practices have left many developing countries struggling to escape the cycle of poverty and limited economic opportunities. Addressing systemic racism is crucial to leveling the playing field and promoting global economic justice.

Gender and Racial Income Inequality:

Systemic racism intersects with gender disparities, resulting in compounded income inequality for women of color. Women of racial minorities face multiple barriers, including wage gaps, limited job prospects, and discrimination, making it imperative to address the unique challenges they face in the pursuit of economic empowerment.

Education and Healthcare Access:

Systemic racism perpetuates unequal access to quality education and healthcare. Racial minorities often face limited resources, substandard schools, and inadequate healthcare facilities, hindering their ability to secure well-paying jobs and maintain good health.

Developing and Developed Countries:

Income inequality in developing countries is exacerbated by systemic racism, as racial minorities are often denied equal access to education, healthcare, and employment opportunities. Developed countries also grapple with racial income disparities, as systemic racism perpetuates biases in hiring, promotions, and wage structures.

Urban and Rural Areas:

Systemic racism manifests differently in urban and rural areas, with racial minorities facing unique challenges in both settings. Urban areas often concentrate poverty, limited job prospects, and inadequate public services, while rural areas face issues such as limited access to education, healthcare, and infrastructure, all of which contribute to income disparities.

The Tech Industry and the Gig Economy:

The tech industry and the gig economy have gained prominence in recent years, but systemic racism persists within these sectors. Racial minority individuals often face barriers in accessing tech education and employment opportunities, while gig workers, who are predominately racial minorities, frequently experience precarious working conditions and low wages.

Conclusion:

The impact of systemic racism on income inequality cannot be ignored. Addressing this issue requires systemic changes, including policies promoting equal opportunities, access to quality education and healthcare, and dismantling discriminatory practices in all sectors. By acknowledging the unique challenges faced by racial minorities in various niches, politicians can take meaningful action to create a more equitable society for all.

Promoting Racial Economic Equity

In recent years, the issue of racial economic equity has gained significant attention worldwide. As politicians, it is our responsibility to address this pressing concern and take decisive action to rectify the existing disparities. This subchapter aims to shed light on the various dimensions of racial income inequality and provide feasible solutions that can foster a more equitable society.

Racial income inequality is a pervasive problem that affects individuals and communities across the globe. It is rooted in historical disadvantage, systemic racism, and unequal distribution of resources. To combat this issue, we must first acknowledge the existence of racial economic disparities and commit ourselves to rectifying them.

One crucial aspect of promoting racial economic equity is addressing the underlying causes of income inequality. This includes dismantling discriminatory policies, ensuring equal access to quality education and healthcare, and promoting fair employment practices. By focusing on these areas, we can create a more inclusive society where individuals from all racial backgrounds have equal opportunities to succeed.

Education plays a pivotal role in breaking the cycle of intergenerational poverty and promoting upward mobility. Investing in quality education in underserved communities is essential to equip individuals with the skills and knowledge needed to compete in today's global economy. Additionally, we must work towards eliminating racial disparities in access to higher education, scholarships, and vocational training programs.

Access to affordable and quality healthcare is another critical aspect of promoting racial economic equity. Racial minorities often face barriers in accessing healthcare services, leading to disparities in health outcomes. By addressing these disparities and ensuring equal access to healthcare, we can improve the overall well-being and productivity of individuals, regardless of their racial background.

Furthermore, it is essential to create an inclusive economy that provides equal opportunities for all, regardless of race. This involves promoting diversity and inclusivity in the tech industry and the gig economy, where racial disparities are often prevalent. By implementing policies that encourage fair hiring practices, equal pay, and career advancement opportunities, we can foster an environment that values and rewards talent regardless of race.

Finally, we must recognize that racial economic equity is not limited to urban areas but also affects rural communities. Investing in infrastructure, job creation, and sustainable development in rural areas can help bridge the income gap and ensure that no community is left behind.

In conclusion, promoting racial economic equity requires a comprehensive approach that addresses the root causes of income inequality. By dismantling discriminatory systems, improving access to education and healthcare, and fostering an inclusive economy, we can create a fair and just society where individuals from all racial backgrounds have equal opportunities to thrive. As politicians, it is our duty to champion these causes and work towards building a more equitable world.

Chapter 5: Income Inequality in Education

Education as a Catalyst for Social Mobility

In today's world, where income inequality continues to persist and hinder social progress, education stands as a powerful catalyst for achieving social mobility and addressing the various forms of inequality that plague our societies. As politicians, it is crucial to recognize the transformative potential of education in combating world's income inequality, gender income inequality, racial income inequality, income inequality in education, income inequality in healthcare access, income inequality in developing and developed countries, income inequality in urban and rural areas, income inequality in the tech industry, and income inequality in the gig economy.

Education has the ability to break the cycle of poverty and provide individuals with the tools and knowledge necessary to improve their economic prospects. By investing in quality education, particularly in underserved communities, politicians can directly tackle income inequality at its root. Equal access to education, regardless of socioeconomic background, race, or gender, is essential to leveling the playing field and creating a fairer society. This means ensuring that quality education is affordable, adequately funded, and accessible to all.

Furthermore, education plays a vital role in addressing gender income inequality. By providing girls and women with equal educational opportunities, we can empower them to pursue higher-paying careers, challenge gender stereotypes, and dismantle the barriers that limit their economic potential. Investing in girls' education is not only a matter of social justice but also an economic imperative that can yield substantial returns for societies as a whole.

Similarly, education has the power to combat racial income inequality. By promoting inclusive and diverse educational environments, politicians can foster social cohesion, promote understanding, and dismantle systemic barriers that perpetuate racial disparities. Additionally, education can equip marginalized communities with the skills and knowledge needed to thrive in a rapidly changing world, thereby reducing the income gap.

It is also essential to recognize the role of education in addressing income inequality in healthcare access. By promoting health literacy and providing education on preventive healthcare measures, individuals can be empowered to make informed decisions regarding their health. Access to quality healthcare and education go hand in hand, and by ensuring that all individuals have access to both, politicians can make significant strides in reducing income-based disparities in healthcare outcomes.

In developing countries, where income inequality is often more pronounced, education holds the key to unlocking economic growth and social progress. By investing in education infrastructure, training qualified teachers, and expanding educational opportunities, politicians can break the cycle of poverty and create a more equitable society. Similarly, in developed countries, education remains a crucial tool for addressing income inequality and ensuring that economic prosperity is shared by all.

In urban and rural areas alike, education can serve as a bridge to social mobility. By investing in schools in rural communities and providing equal opportunities for quality education, politicians can empower individuals living in these areas to overcome the challenges associated with limited resources and access to opportunities. Similarly, in urban areas, education can provide marginalized communities with the skills needed to compete in the job market and escape poverty.

The tech industry and the gig economy are not immune to income inequality. By promoting digital literacy and providing educational programs that equip individuals with the skills needed in these sectors, politicians can ensure that no one is left behind in the digital revolution. Education can help bridge the digital divide and create opportunities for individuals to participate in and benefit from the tech industry and the gig economy.

In conclusion, education stands as a crucial catalyst for social mobility and a powerful tool for addressing income inequality in all its manifestations. As politicians, it is our responsibility to prioritize education as a means to promote social progress, bridge income gaps, and create a fairer and more equitable society. By investing in quality education, ensuring equal access, and empowering individuals with the skills and knowledge needed to thrive, we can truly make a difference in the lives of our citizens and build a more inclusive future for all.

The Achievement Gap and its Relation to Income

Income inequality is a pressing issue that affects various aspects of society, including education. In this subchapter, we will explore the relationship between income and the achievement gap. The achievement gap refers to the disparities in educational outcomes among different groups, such as racial or ethnic minorities, low-income students, and those from disadvantaged backgrounds.

Research has consistently shown that there is a strong correlation between income and educational achievement. Students from lower-income households tend to have lower educational attainment compared to their wealthier counterparts. This gap becomes particularly apparent in standardized test scores, graduation rates, and college enrollment rates.

One of the main reasons for this correlation is the unequal access to quality educational resources. Affluent families can afford to live in neighborhoods with well-funded schools, hire tutors, and provide enrichment activities for their children. On the other hand, low-income families often face limited resources, overcrowded classrooms, and a lack of extracurricular opportunities. These disparities exacerbate the achievement gap and perpetuate the cycle of inequality.

Moreover, income inequality also affects the quality of teaching. Teachers in low-income schools often face more challenging working conditions, such as larger class sizes, higher student turnover, and fewer resources. As a result, these schools struggle to attract and retain qualified and experienced teachers, further widening the achievement gap.

Addressing the achievement gap requires a comprehensive approach that tackles income inequality. Policymakers must prioritize equitable funding for schools, ensuring that resources are distributed based on the needs of students and not solely on property taxes. Additionally, targeted interventions, such as early childhood education programs and mentorship initiatives, can help level the playing field for disadvantaged students.

Furthermore, investing in teacher training and professional development in low-income schools is crucial. By providing teachers with the necessary support and resources, we can enhance the quality of education and bridge the achievement gap.

In conclusion, the achievement gap is closely intertwined with income inequality. To create a more equitable education system, politicians must recognize the impact of income disparities on educational outcomes. By addressing income inequality and implementing targeted policies, we can work towards narrowing the achievement gap and providing equal opportunities for all students, regardless of their socioeconomic background.

Policy Interventions for Equal Educational Opportunities

One of the most effective ways to address income inequality is through policy interventions that aim to provide equal educational opportunities for all. Education is a powerful tool that can help individuals overcome the disadvantages they face due to their socioeconomic background, gender, race, or geographic location. By investing in education and ensuring that every individual has access to high-quality education, policymakers can help level the playing field and promote social mobility.

To tackle income inequality in education, policymakers should prioritize several key interventions. First and foremost, it is essential to invest in early childhood education. Research has consistently shown that high-quality early childhood education programs have long-lasting positive effects on children's cognitive and social development. By providing children from disadvantaged backgrounds with access to quality early education, policymakers can help narrow the achievement gap from the start.

Additionally, policymakers should focus on improving the quality of primary and secondary education in marginalized communities. This can be achieved by increasing funding for schools in low-income areas, attracting and retaining highly qualified teachers, and implementing evidence-based teaching practices. By improving the quality of education in marginalized communities, policymakers can ensure that all students have an equal chance to succeed academically.

Furthermore, policymakers should consider implementing affirmative action policies to promote diversity and inclusion in higher education. This can help address the underrepresentation of certain marginalized groups in colleges and universities. Affirmative action can play a crucial role in creating a more equitable society by providing opportunities for historically disadvantaged individuals.

Moreover, policymakers should prioritize vocational training and skills development programs. Not all individuals are suited for traditional academic paths, and providing alternative avenues for skill acquisition can help bridge the income gap. By investing in vocational training and apprenticeship programs, policymakers can equip individuals with the skills necessary to secure well-paying jobs and contribute to the economy.

In conclusion, policy interventions for equal educational opportunities are crucial to address income inequality. By investing in early childhood education, improving the quality of primary and secondary education in marginalized communities, implementing affirmative action policies, and prioritizing vocational training programs, policymakers can create a more equitable society. It is imperative for politicians to recognize the transformative power of education and take concrete steps to ensure that every individual has equal access to high-quality education, regardless of their background or circumstances. By doing so, they can pave the way for a more inclusive and prosperous future for all.

Chapter 6: Income Inequality in Healthcare Access

Healthcare Disparities and Income Inequality

Introduction

In today's globalized and interconnected world, income inequality remains a pressing issue that affects various aspects of society. One critical area where income inequality manifests itself is in healthcare disparities. Access to quality healthcare is not only a basic human right but also a fundamental determinant of societal well-being and economic growth. This subchapter will explore the intersection between income inequality and healthcare disparities, shedding light on the challenges faced by various populations across the world, including those in developing and developed countries, rural and urban areas, and specific industries such as the tech sector and gig economy.

The Impact of Income Inequality on Healthcare Access

Income inequality significantly affects healthcare access, resulting in disparities that disproportionately affect marginalized populations. World's income inequality, gender income inequality, racial income inequality, and income inequality in education all contribute to unequal access to healthcare services. Lower-income individuals and communities often struggle to afford health insurance, medications, and preventative care, leading to poorer health outcomes and increased healthcare costs in the long run.

Disparities in Developing and Developed Countries

Income inequality in healthcare access is a significant challenge in both developing and developed countries. In developing countries, limited resources and infrastructure hinder access to essential healthcare services, exacerbating health disparities. In developed countries, income inequality leads to unequal access to healthcare even within well-established systems, as lower-income individuals face barriers such as high insurance costs and limited healthcare facilities in their neighborhoods.

Urban-Rural Divide

Income inequality in healthcare access is also evident in the urban-rural divide. Rural areas often lack adequate healthcare infrastructure, including hospitals, clinics, and specialized healthcare professionals. Limited transportation options further hinder access to healthcare services for rural populations, exacerbating disparities in health outcomes between urban and rural areas.

Income Inequality in Specific Industries

Income inequality is not limited to geographical or demographic factors. Within specific industries like the tech sector and gig economy, disparities in income can impact healthcare access. Workers in the gig economy often lack access to employer-provided health insurance, leaving them more vulnerable to health problems. Similarly, income disparities in the tech industry can affect the ability of lower-income employees to afford quality healthcare services.

Conclusion

Addressing healthcare disparities caused by income inequality requires a multi-faceted approach. Policymakers must prioritize reducing income inequality through progressive taxation, improved access to education, and targeted social welfare programs. Additionally, investments in healthcare infrastructure and the expansion of affordable healthcare options are essential to ensure equal access to quality healthcare for all. By addressing healthcare disparities and income inequality, policymakers can promote a more equitable society that fosters the well-being and prosperity of all individuals, regardless of their income or social status.

Implications of Limited Healthcare Access

Access to adequate healthcare is a fundamental human right, yet it remains an elusive privilege for millions of people around the world. This subchapter aims to shed light on the far-reaching implications of limited healthcare access, urging politicians to take immediate action to address this pressing issue. By understanding the broader consequences of unequal access to healthcare, policymakers can devise effective strategies to reduce income inequality and promote social progress.

Limited healthcare access has profound implications for several dimensions of inequality. Firstly, in terms of world income inequality, lack of access to healthcare perpetuates a vicious cycle of poverty and ill-health, particularly in developing countries. The inability to afford medical services and treatments further exacerbates income disparities, leaving the marginalized even more vulnerable.

Gender income inequality is also intertwined with limited healthcare access. Women often face greater challenges in accessing healthcare due to systemic gender biases, cultural barriers, and discriminatory practices. Inadequate access to reproductive healthcare and maternal care not only affects women's health but also hinders their economic empowerment and overall well-being.

Similarly, racial income inequality is closely linked to limited healthcare access. Minority communities often face systemic barriers that prevent them from accessing quality healthcare services. This perpetuates health disparities and reinforces racial income gaps, leading to a vicious cycle of disadvantage.

Furthermore, income inequality in education and healthcare access are closely interconnected. Limited access to healthcare disproportionately affects children from low-income families, hindering their overall educational attainment and future prospects. This creates a perpetual cycle of poverty and inequality, limiting social mobility and economic progress.

In both developed and developing countries, income inequality is starkly evident in urban and rural areas. Limited healthcare access in rural areas often results in higher mortality rates, reduced life expectancy, and limited economic opportunities. Meanwhile, income inequality in urban areas is manifested through disparities in access to healthcare facilities, with marginalized communities often lacking basic healthcare infrastructure.

The tech industry and the gig economy also contribute to income inequality, with limited healthcare access being a significant concern. Many gig workers lack access to employer-provided healthcare benefits, leaving them vulnerable to financial hardship and limited access to medical services. This exacerbates income disparities, as those with higher-paying tech jobs often have better access to healthcare benefits.

In conclusion, limited healthcare access has far-reaching implications for various dimensions of income inequality. By recognizing these implications, politicians can prioritize healthcare reform and allocate resources to ensure equitable access to healthcare for all. Addressing healthcare disparities is not only a moral imperative but also an essential step towards reducing income inequality, promoting social justice, and fostering inclusive economic growth.

Strategies for Achieving Healthcare Equity

In recent years, the issue of healthcare equity has gained significant attention worldwide. Access to quality healthcare is a fundamental human right, yet it remains elusive for millions of individuals across the globe. Addressing healthcare equity is not only a matter of social justice but also has significant economic implications. In this subchapter, we will explore various strategies that politicians can implement to achieve healthcare equity, with a focus on the different niches affected by income inequality.

1. Universal healthcare coverage: One of the most effective ways to achieve healthcare equity is by implementing universal healthcare coverage. This system ensures that every individual, regardless of their income or social status, has access to essential healthcare services. Politicians should prioritize the establishment of comprehensive healthcare systems that cover the entire population, reducing the disparities in healthcare access.

2. Reducing healthcare costs: High healthcare costs often lead to significant barriers to access, particularly for those with lower incomes. Policymakers should strive to implement measures that reduce the cost burden on individuals, such as negotiating drug prices, promoting generic drugs, and implementing cost-control measures within the healthcare industry.

3. Improving healthcare infrastructure: In many developing countries and rural areas, lack of proper healthcare infrastructure hinders access to quality healthcare. Politicians should prioritize investments in healthcare infrastructure, including the construction of hospitals, clinics, and medical facilities in underserved regions.

4. Addressing social determinants of health: Income inequality is closely associated with various social determinants of health, such as education, housing, and employment. Policymakers should develop holistic approaches that address these determinants and reduce their impact on healthcare access. This can include initiatives such as improving educational opportunities, providing affordable housing, and promoting job creation in disadvantaged areas.

5. Health education and awareness: Promoting health education and awareness campaigns can empower individuals to take control of their health and reduce healthcare disparities. Politicians should support initiatives that provide accurate health information, promote preventive care, and raise awareness about available healthcare services.

6. Targeted interventions: In order to address specific niches affected by income inequality, politicians should implement targeted interventions. For example, in the tech industry, where income disparities are prevalent, policies could be developed to ensure fair wages and benefits for all employees, regardless of their job positions or contracts.

Achieving healthcare equity requires a comprehensive and multi-faceted approach. By implementing these strategies and tailoring them to specific niches affected by income inequality, politicians can work towards a society where access to quality healthcare is a reality for all individuals, regardless of their income or social status. It is through these concerted efforts that we can create a fairer and more equitable healthcare system, improving the well-being of all citizens and driving economic growth.

Chapter 7: Income Inequality in Developing Countries

Challenges Faced by Developing Nations

In today's globalized world, developing nations face a myriad of challenges that hinder their economic growth and perpetuate income inequality. The subchapter "Challenges Faced by Developing Nations" aims to shed light on these obstacles and provide a call to action for politicians to address them effectively.

One of the most pressing issues faced by developing nations is world income inequality. The gap between the rich and the poor has widened significantly over the years, posing a threat to social cohesion and sustainable development. Politicians must recognize this disparity and implement policies that promote inclusive growth, such as progressive taxation and investment in social programs.

Gender income inequality is another critical challenge faced by developing nations. Women continue to earn less than men for the same work, limiting their economic opportunities and perpetuating gender-based discrimination. Policymakers must prioritize gender equality, ensuring equal pay and access to education and healthcare for women.

Similarly, racial income inequality persists as a significant obstacle in many developing nations. Ethnic minorities often face discrimination and limited access to resources, hindering their socio-economic mobility. Politicians must work towards dismantling systemic racism and promoting equal opportunities for all citizens.

Education and healthcare are fundamental rights that should be accessible to all. However, income inequality often translates into unequal access to quality education and healthcare services in developing nations. Politicians must invest in public education and healthcare systems, ensuring that every citizen, regardless of their socio-economic background, can access these essential services.

While income inequality is prevalent in both developing and developed nations, the challenges faced by developing countries are often more severe. Limited access to resources, infrastructure, and technology further exacerbates income disparities. Policymakers must focus on promoting inclusive economic growth, providing opportunities for job creation, and investing in sustainable development.

Income inequality is not limited to urban areas; rural regions also face unique challenges. Lack of infrastructure, limited job opportunities, and inadequate access to education and healthcare contribute to the perpetuation of income disparities. Politicians must implement policies that bridge the rural-urban divide and ensure equitable development across all regions.

The tech industry and the gig economy have emerged as major drivers of economic growth globally. However, income inequality within these sectors is a growing concern. Politicians must regulate these industries to prevent unfair labor practices and ensure that the benefits of technological advancements are distributed equitably.

In conclusion, developing nations face numerous challenges that perpetuate income inequality. As policymakers, politicians must address these challenges by implementing progressive policies, promoting gender and racial equality, investing in education and healthcare, and bridging the rural-urban divide. By taking proactive measures, politicians can pave the way for inclusive economic growth and create a more equitable society for all citizens.

Factors Contributing to Income Inequality in Developing Countries

Income inequality is a pervasive issue that affects societies across the globe. In developing countries, this disparity is particularly pronounced and presents numerous challenges for policymakers. This subchapter aims to shed light on the factors contributing to income inequality in developing countries, providing a comprehensive understanding of the underlying causes and potential solutions to address this pressing issue.

1. Unequal distribution of resources: One of the primary drivers of income inequality in developing countries is the unequal distribution of resources. Limited access to education, healthcare, and basic services disproportionately affects the marginalized populations, perpetuating a cycle of poverty and income inequality.

2. Lack of economic opportunities: Developing countries often struggle with limited economic opportunities, leading to a concentration of wealth in the hands of a few individuals or corporations. Insufficient job creation, inadequate infrastructure, and limited access to credit exacerbate income inequality by excluding large segments of the population from participating in economic growth.

3. Corruption and weak governance: Corruption and weak governance contribute significantly to income inequality in developing countries. When government officials engage in corrupt practices, public resources meant for societal development are diverted, leaving the most vulnerable populations without essential services and further widening the income gap.

4. Global economic policies: The impact of global economic policies on developing countries cannot be overlooked. Unfair trade practices, unfavorable terms of trade, and excessive debt burdens imposed by international financial institutions can hinder economic growth and perpetuate income inequality.

5. Social and cultural factors: Social and cultural factors, such as gender and racial discrimination, also play a significant role in income inequality. In many developing countries, women and minority groups face significant barriers to accessing education, employment, and equal opportunities, leading to a persistent income gap.

Addressing income inequality in developing countries requires a multi-faceted approach that tackles these underlying factors. Policymakers should focus on implementing inclusive economic policies that promote job creation, invest in education and healthcare, and ensure equal access to resources. Additionally, efforts to combat corruption and strengthen governance structures are crucial to creating a level playing field for all citizens.

Furthermore, international cooperation and fair global economic policies are essential in addressing income inequality in developing countries. Developed nations should strive to create a more equitable trading system, provide debt relief, and support sustainable development initiatives to empower developing countries to overcome the challenges of income inequality.

In conclusion, income inequality in developing countries is a complex issue influenced by various factors. Policymakers must recognize and address the unequal distribution of resources, limited economic opportunities, corruption, global economic policies, and social and cultural barriers to create a more inclusive and equitable society. By taking action to mitigate these factors, politicians can pave the way for sustainable economic development and social progress in developing countries.

Promoting Sustainable Development and Reducing Inequality

Promoting Sustainable Development and Reducing Inequality: A Call to Action for Politicians

Introduction:

In recent years, the issue of income inequality has become a pressing concern globally. The disparities in wealth and opportunities have reached alarming levels, affecting various aspects of society, from education and healthcare to urban and rural areas. As politicians, it is our responsibility to address these inequalities and work towards sustainable development that ensures a more equitable future for all. This subchapter aims to shed light on the key areas where income inequality persists and emphasizes the urgent need for action.

World's Income Inequality:

Income inequality is not confined to a specific region or country; it is a global challenge. The concentration of wealth in the hands of a few has far-reaching consequences, including social unrest, political instability, and hindered economic growth. As politicians, we must collaborate on a global scale to implement policies that promote fair income distribution and bridge the wealth gap.

Gender, Racial, and Educational Income Inequality:

Income inequality is particularly pronounced when it comes to gender and racial disparities. Women and minority groups often face lower pay and limited access to opportunities, perpetuating a cycle of inequality. Additionally, income disparities in education further exacerbate this issue, as the lack of equal opportunities hinders social mobility and perpetuates intergenerational poverty. Policymakers must prioritize gender pay equity, eliminate racial disparities, and invest in education to break these cycles of inequality.

Healthcare Access and Development:

Income inequality also influences access to healthcare, with the poorest individuals being disproportionately affected by inadequate medical care. This disparity not only affects individuals' well-being but also undermines a nation's overall development. Policymakers must strive to ensure equal access to healthcare, regardless of income, and invest in public health infrastructure to bridge this gap.

Developed vs. Developing Countries:

While income inequality is prevalent in both developed and developing countries, the challenges they face are distinct. Developed nations must focus on addressing wealth concentration and ensuring that economic growth benefits all citizens. In contrast, developing countries must prioritize poverty reduction, inclusive growth, and creating opportunities for disadvantaged populations.

Urban vs. Rural Income Inequality:

Income inequality manifests differently in urban and rural areas. Urban areas often witness higher income inequality due to the concentration of economic opportunities, while rural areas face challenges such as limited access to resources and services. Policymakers need to design region-specific strategies that address the unique needs of both urban and rural populations.

Income Inequality in the Tech Industry and Gig Economy:

The rapid growth of the tech industry and the gig economy has created new dimensions of income inequality. Technological advancements have resulted in job displacement, leaving many workers in precarious employment. Policymakers must ensure that these new industries provide fair wages, benefits, and opportunities for all workers, and protect vulnerable individuals from exploitation.

Conclusion:

Addressing income inequality and promoting sustainable development requires collective action from politicians worldwide. By focusing on key areas such as gender, racial, educational, healthcare, and urban-rural income inequality, as well as the challenges in the tech industry and gig economy, we can create a more inclusive and equitable society. The time for action is now, and politicians must lead the way in implementing policies that prioritize reducing inequality and fostering sustainable development for the benefit of all. Let us seize this opportunity and work towards a future where no one is left behind.

Chapter 8: Income Inequality in Developed Countries

Economic Disparities in Advanced Economies

In today's interconnected world, economic disparities continue to persist in advanced economies, posing significant challenges for politicians and policymakers. This subchapter delves into the complex and multifaceted nature of economic inequality, shedding light on various dimensions and their impact on different sections of society.

1. World's Income Inequality: Despite advancements in technology and globalization, income inequality remains a pressing issue on a global scale. Politicians must recognize the significance of global cooperation to address this disparity, as the consequences of income inequality transcend national borders.

2. Gender Income Inequality: Gender disparities in income are prevalent across advanced economies. It is crucial for politicians to acknowledge the gender pay gap and take action to ensure equal opportunities and fair compensation for women in the workforce.

3. Racial Income Inequality: Income disparities based on race persist in advanced economies, perpetuating systemic discrimination and hindering social progress. Policymakers must confront racial income inequality head-on, implementing policies that promote inclusivity, equal opportunities, and address historical disadvantages.

4. Income Inequality in Education: Education is a fundamental driver for upward mobility and reducing income inequality. However, disparities in access to quality education hinder social mobility. Politicians need to prioritize educational reforms, ensuring that every

individual has an equal chance to succeed regardless of their socio-economic background.

5. Income Inequality in Healthcare Access: Access to healthcare services is a basic human right, yet income inequalities often determine the quality and availability of healthcare. Politicians must strive to create equitable healthcare systems that guarantee affordable and accessible services to all citizens.

6. Income Inequality in Developing Countries: Developing countries face unique challenges in combating income inequality. Politicians must focus on inclusive growth strategies, promoting sustainable development, and reducing poverty to bridge the income gap.

7. Income Inequality in Developed Countries: Advanced economies are not immune to income inequality. Politicians must address the growing wealth gap, implement progressive tax policies, and invest in social safety nets to ensure a fairer distribution of resources.

8. Income Inequality in Urban Areas: Urban areas often witness higher income disparities due to factors such as rising housing costs and unequal job opportunities. Policymakers must prioritize urban development policies that promote affordable housing, job creation, and social integration.

9. Income Inequality in Rural Areas: Rural communities often face unique challenges in terms of income inequality, such as limited access to resources and services. Politicians must focus on rural development initiatives, including investment in infrastructure, education, and agricultural reforms to uplift these communities.

10. Income Inequality in the Tech Industry: The tech industry has witnessed significant wealth accumulation, leading to income disparities. Policymakers must regulate the industry, ensure fair taxation, and

promote inclusive hiring practices to address income inequality in this sector.

11. Income Inequality in the Gig Economy: The rise of the gig economy has brought new challenges, including income instability and lack of benefits for gig workers. Politicians should strive to create regulations that protect gig workers' rights, ensure fair compensation, and provide social safety nets.

In conclusion, economic disparities in advanced economies span a wide range of areas, posing significant challenges for politicians. Addressing these disparities requires a comprehensive and multi-dimensional approach, focusing on policies that promote equal opportunities, inclusive growth, and social justice. By understanding the nuances of income inequality in different niches, policymakers can formulate effective strategies to create a fairer and more equitable society.

Causes and Consequences of Income Inequality in Developed Countries

Introduction:

Income inequality has become an increasingly pressing issue in developed countries over the past few decades. The gap between the rich and the poor has widened significantly, leading to various social and economic consequences. This subchapter aims to shed light on the causes and consequences of income inequality in developed countries, urging politicians to take action and address this issue effectively.

Causes of Income Inequality:

1. Technological Advancements: Rapid technological progress has led to the automation of many jobs, resulting in a decline in employment opportunities for low-skilled workers. This has contributed to a widening income gap between those with advanced skills and those without.

2. Globalization: The integration of economies through globalization has led to the outsourcing of jobs to countries with lower labor costs. This has affected the job market in developed countries, particularly in manufacturing sectors, leading to job losses and wage stagnation for many workers.

3. Tax Policies: Tax policies that favor the wealthy, such as lower tax rates on capital gains and dividends, have contributed to income inequality. These policies often benefit the rich disproportionately, resulting in a concentration of wealth among a small portion of the population.

Consequences of Income Inequality:

1. Social Cohesion: High levels of income inequality can lead to social unrest and a breakdown in social cohesion. The gap between the rich and the poor can create resentment and a sense of injustice, leading to social divisions and a lack of trust in institutions.

2. Health Disparities: Income inequality is closely linked to disparities in health outcomes. Lower-income individuals often have limited access to quality healthcare, leading to higher rates of chronic illnesses and shorter life expectancies compared to their wealthier counterparts.

3. Education Disparities: Income inequality affects access to quality education. Children from low-income families often lack the resources and opportunities necessary for academic success, perpetuating intergenerational poverty and limiting social mobility.

4. Economic Growth: High levels of income inequality can hinder economic growth. When wealth is concentrated in the hands of a few, it limits consumer spending and investment, leading to a sluggish economy.

Conclusion:

Addressing income inequality should be a priority for politicians in developed countries. By implementing policies that promote equal opportunities, such as investing in education and training programs, raising the minimum wage, and reforming tax policies, politicians can help reduce income inequality and create a more equitable society. Additionally, addressing income inequality can lead to improved social cohesion, better health outcomes, and stronger economic growth. It is crucial that politicians take action to bridge the gap between the rich and the poor, ensuring a fair and prosperous society for all citizens.

Policies to Address Income Inequality in Developed Nations

Income inequality remains a pressing issue in developed nations across the globe, affecting various aspects of society, including gender, race, education, healthcare access, and urban and rural areas. As politicians, it is crucial to understand the depth of this problem and implement effective policies to address it. In this subchapter, we will explore a range of strategies aimed at reducing income inequality in developed nations.

One of the key areas where income inequality persists is in the world of work. To combat this, policymakers should focus on promoting fair wages and improving the rights of workers. Implementing a minimum wage that is both adequate and adjusted for inflation can help ensure that individuals earn a living wage. Additionally, strengthening labor unions and collective bargaining rights can provide workers with a stronger voice in negotiating wages and working conditions.

Gender and racial income inequality are also pervasive issues that require targeted policies. Encouraging equal pay for equal work and addressing discriminatory practices in hiring and promotions are essential steps toward achieving gender and racial income equality. Affirmative action policies can promote diversity and inclusion, ensuring that historically marginalized groups have equal opportunities to access high-paying jobs and positions of power.

Furthermore, investing in education and healthcare is crucial for reducing income inequality. Providing quality education regardless of socioeconomic background can help level the playing field and create equal opportunities for all. Implementing progressive tax policies and increasing government spending on education can ensure that even the most disadvantaged individuals have access to quality schooling.

Similarly, ensuring equal access to healthcare is vital for reducing income inequality. Expanding healthcare coverage and implementing universal healthcare systems can guarantee that everyone, regardless of income, has access to necessary medical care. This can prevent individuals from falling into poverty due to healthcare expenses and provide a more equitable society.

Addressing income inequality in both urban and rural areas is essential for achieving balanced development. Policies that promote affordable housing, improve infrastructure, and provide support for small businesses in rural areas can help reduce disparities between urban and rural communities.

In addition to these strategies, it is essential to address income inequality in specific industries such as the tech industry and the gig economy. Implementing regulations to ensure fair wages, benefits, and worker protections in these sectors can help reduce income disparities and promote a more inclusive economy.

In conclusion, income inequality is a complex issue that affects various aspects of society. Policymakers must take bold action to address this problem. By implementing policies that promote fair wages, equal opportunities, quality education, accessible healthcare, and balanced development, politicians can begin to combat income inequality in developed nations and create a more just and equitable society for all.

Chapter 9: Income Inequality in Urban Areas

Urbanization and Income Disparities

As the world becomes increasingly urbanized, the issue of income disparities takes center stage. Urbanization, defined as the process of population migration from rural to urban areas, has significant implications for income inequality across various dimensions. In this subchapter, we will explore the intersection of urbanization and income disparities, shedding light on its impact on the world's income inequality, gender income inequality, racial income inequality, income inequality in education, income inequality in healthcare access, income inequality in developing countries, income inequality in developed countries, income inequality in urban areas, income inequality in rural areas, income inequality in the tech industry, and income inequality in the gig economy.

Urban areas often attract individuals seeking better economic opportunities, resulting in concentrated wealth and socioeconomic disparities. This pattern is evident in both developed and developing countries. In developed countries, urban centers tend to host high-paying jobs in sectors such as finance, technology, and professional services, leading to income disparities between urban and rural areas. On the other hand, developing countries face challenges related to rapid urbanization, where inadequate infrastructure and limited job opportunities can exacerbate income disparities within urban areas.

Moreover, urbanization intersects with various dimensions of income inequality, including gender, race, and education. Women, for instance, often face greater income disparities in urban areas due to factors such as gender bias, occupational segregation, and limited access to quality education and healthcare. Similarly, racial income disparities are often pronounced in urban settings, where historical and structural factors perpetuate unequal opportunities for minority populations.

Education and healthcare access are crucial determinants of income disparities, and urbanization plays a significant role in shaping these dynamics. Urban areas may have better educational and healthcare facilities, but access to these services can be limited for low-income individuals, perpetuating income disparities. Additionally, income inequality in the tech industry and the gig economy is often concentrated in urban areas, where high-skilled workers benefit while low-skilled workers struggle to earn a living wage.

To address these challenges, policymakers must prioritize inclusive urban development strategies. Investments in education, healthcare, infrastructure, and affordable housing are essential to mitigate income disparities in urban areas. Moreover, targeted policies addressing gender and racial income disparities can help create a more equitable urban environment.

In conclusion, urbanization is a significant driver of income disparities across various dimensions. Policymakers must recognize the intersectionality of income inequality in urban areas and implement measures to foster inclusive growth. By addressing the specific challenges faced by different groups within urban settings, we can strive towards a more equitable society, ensuring that the benefits of urbanization are shared by all.

Urban Poverty and Social Exclusion

In recent years, the issue of urban poverty and social exclusion has become increasingly prominent in political discussions. As politicians, it is crucial to understand the various dimensions of this complex problem and devise effective strategies to tackle it. This subchapter aims to shed light on the causes and consequences of urban poverty and social exclusion, while also exploring potential policy interventions.

Urban areas are often seen as hubs of economic growth and innovation. However, within these bustling cities, stark inequalities persist, leading to the marginalization of certain groups. World's Income Inequality, Gender income inequality, Racial income inequality, and Income inequality in education are just a few of the niches where urban poverty and social exclusion are particularly pronounced.

One of the key drivers of urban poverty is the lack of access to quality education and healthcare. Income inequality in education perpetuates a vicious cycle, where individuals from low-income backgrounds are unable to acquire the necessary skills to secure well-paying jobs. Similarly, income inequality in healthcare access means that marginalized communities often struggle to receive adequate medical care, leading to poorer health outcomes.

Developing countries face unique challenges in addressing urban poverty and social exclusion. Rapid urbanization, coupled with inadequate infrastructure and limited job opportunities, exacerbates inequality. On the other hand, developed countries grapple with issues such as affordable housing and the digital divide, which contribute to urban poverty and exclusion.

Furthermore, income inequality in the tech industry and the gig economy has garnered attention in recent years. The rise of digital platforms and the gig economy has created new income opportunities but also widened existing inequalities. Policymakers must grapple with the need for regulation and social protection in these sectors, ensuring that workers are not left behind.

To tackle urban poverty and social exclusion, a multi-faceted approach is essential. Policymakers can explore strategies such as investing in education and healthcare infrastructure, promoting affordable housing initiatives, and implementing progressive taxation policies. Additionally, targeted programs focusing on skills training, job creation, and social protection can help uplift marginalized communities.

In conclusion, addressing urban poverty and social exclusion requires a comprehensive understanding of the various factors contributing to inequality. By recognizing the specific challenges faced by different niches, policymakers can design targeted interventions to reduce disparities. It is crucial for politicians to act now and prioritize these issues, promoting inclusive growth and ensuring a more equitable society for all.

Urban Planning for Inclusive Growth

In recent years, the issue of income inequality has gained significant attention worldwide. From the World's Income Inequality to Gender, Racial, and Educational income inequalities, it has become clear that addressing these disparities is crucial for the overall well-being of societies. Urban areas, in particular, play a fundamental role in both perpetuating and mitigating income inequality. As politicians, it is imperative to recognize the critical role that urban planning can play in fostering inclusive growth and reducing income disparities.

Income inequality in urban areas is often more pronounced than in rural areas, as cities tend to concentrate both wealth and poverty. However, with effective urban planning, cities can become powerful drivers of inclusive economic growth. By implementing policies that promote affordable housing, access to quality education, healthcare, and job opportunities, urban areas can become engines of social mobility, providing equal opportunities for all residents.

One key aspect of urban planning for inclusive growth is ensuring affordable housing options. Rising housing costs in cities have increasingly excluded low-income individuals and families, exacerbating income inequality. By implementing policies such as rent control, mixed-income housing developments, and affordable housing quotas, politicians can ensure that affordable housing is available to all residents, regardless of their income level.

Another critical area for inclusive urban planning is education. Income inequality in education perpetuates a cycle of disadvantage, limiting opportunities for upward mobility. To address this, politicians should prioritize investments in high-quality public education, ensuring that all children have access to the same educational resources and opportunities. Additionally, initiatives such as scholarships and financial aid programs can help bridge the gap for disadvantaged individuals, leveling the playing field and promoting equal access to higher education.

Furthermore, healthcare access is a fundamental aspect of inclusive urban planning. Income inequality in healthcare access can have severe consequences, as individuals with lower incomes often face barriers to quality healthcare services. Policymakers should work towards implementing universal healthcare systems, ensuring that all residents, regardless of their income, have access to affordable and high-quality healthcare services.

Inclusive urban planning is not limited to developed countries alone. Income inequality in developing countries is often more severe due to various socio-economic factors. However, by adopting inclusive urban planning strategies, politicians in developing countries can create sustainable cities that prioritize the needs of all residents, fostering economic growth and reducing income disparities.

Lastly, the tech industry and gig economy have emerged as significant contributors to income inequality. As politicians, it is essential to regulate these sectors effectively, ensuring fair wages, benefits, and job security for workers. By implementing policies that promote fair labor practices, politicians can help reduce income disparities in these rapidly evolving industries.

In conclusion, urban planning for inclusive growth is a powerful tool to address income inequality in various spheres. By prioritizing affordable housing, education, healthcare access, and fair labor practices, politicians can create cities that provide equal opportunities for all residents. It is crucial to recognize that inclusive urban planning is not a one-size-fits-all approach, as strategies need to be tailored to the specific context and needs of each region. However, with a concerted effort and political will, urban areas can become catalysts for inclusive growth, leading the way towards a more equitable society.

Chapter 10: Income Inequality in Rural Areas

Challenges Faced by Rural Communities

Rural communities across the globe face a myriad of challenges that contribute to income inequality and hinder their economic development. These challenges are multifaceted and require the urgent attention of policymakers and politicians to ensure equitable opportunities and sustainable growth.

One of the primary challenges faced by rural communities is the lack of access to basic infrastructure and essential services. Many rural areas lack reliable electricity, clean water, and proper sanitation facilities. This not only hampers the daily lives of individuals but also inhibits economic activities and limits job prospects. Inadequate transportation networks further isolate rural communities, making it difficult for them to access healthcare, education, and job opportunities in urban areas.

Education is another critical challenge faced by rural communities. Limited access to quality education disproportionately affects rural children, perpetuating a cycle of poverty and inequality. Inadequate funding and lack of qualified teachers in rural schools result in subpar education outcomes. This achievement gap further restricts employment prospects for rural youth, exacerbating income disparities.

Healthcare access is yet another pressing challenge confronted by rural communities. Limited healthcare facilities, a shortage of medical professionals, and long travel distances to reach hospitals and clinics create significant barriers to healthcare services for rural residents. This not only compromises their health but also increases healthcare costs as preventive care is often neglected, resulting in more severe illnesses that require expensive treatments.

Furthermore, rural areas often suffer from a lack of economic diversification and limited job opportunities. Traditional agricultural activities, while important, may not be sufficient to sustain a robust local economy. The absence of industries and businesses in rural areas leads to high unemployment rates and a heavy reliance on government assistance. This perpetuates income inequality and hinders the overall development of rural communities.

Addressing these challenges requires a comprehensive approach that includes targeted investments in rural infrastructure, improving access to quality education and healthcare, and fostering economic diversification. Policymakers must prioritize the development of rural areas by investing in reliable and affordable transportation, expanding broadband connectivity, and providing financial incentives for businesses to establish operations in rural communities.

By addressing the challenges faced by rural communities, policymakers can help bridge the income inequality gap, promote sustainable economic growth, and ensure a more equitable society. It is imperative for politicians to recognize the importance of equal opportunities for all citizens, regardless of their geographical location, and take decisive action to uplift rural communities and create a more inclusive and prosperous society.

Agricultural Sector and Income Inequality

The agricultural sector plays a significant role in shaping income inequality across various dimensions, including gender, race, education, healthcare access, and geography. As politicians, it is crucial to understand the dynamics within this sector and implement policies that address the disparities and promote a more equitable society.

In many developing countries, the agricultural sector is the primary source of employment and income for a significant portion of the population. However, it is also one of the most unequal sectors in terms of income distribution. This inequality is often driven by factors such as land ownership concentration, limited access to credit and resources, and lack of technological advancements. To tackle this issue, policymakers must focus on land reform, providing access to credit and resources, and investing in rural infrastructure and agricultural research and development.

Gender income inequality is another pressing issue within the agricultural sector. Women make up a substantial part of the agricultural workforce but face numerous barriers that limit their access to resources, markets, and decision-making power. Addressing gender disparities in agriculture requires targeted interventions, including promoting women's land rights, providing access to financial services tailored to their needs, and investing in gender-responsive agricultural extension services and training.

Racial income inequality within the agricultural sector is a consequence of historical and structural factors that have disproportionately affected marginalized communities. Policies aimed at reducing racial income disparities in agriculture should focus on increasing access to land, credit, and technical assistance for minority farmers, promoting inclusive agricultural education and training programs, and fostering partnerships with minority-owned businesses and organizations.

Income inequality in education and healthcare access is closely linked to the agricultural sector, particularly in rural areas. Insufficient income and limited access to quality education and healthcare services perpetuate the cycle of poverty and inequality. Policymakers must invest in rural education infrastructure, improve access to quality healthcare, and prioritize initiatives that address the specific needs of rural communities.

In developed countries, income inequality in the agricultural sector may manifest differently, with small-scale farmers facing challenges from large agribusinesses and global market forces. Supporting small-scale farmers through policies that promote local and sustainable agriculture, fair trade practices, and access to markets can help reduce income disparities in this sector.

Furthermore, income inequality in the tech industry and gig economy is closely tied to the agricultural sector, as technology and online platforms are increasingly used in agricultural production and marketing. Policymakers must ensure that the benefits of technological advancements are shared equitably, providing training opportunities and support for farmers to adopt new technologies, and protecting the rights and well-being of workers in the gig economy.

In conclusion, addressing income inequality in the agricultural sector requires a comprehensive and multi-dimensional approach. By understanding the specific challenges faced by different groups and regions, policymakers can implement targeted interventions that promote inclusive growth, reduce disparities, and create a more equitable society.

Empowering Rural Economies for Balanced Growth

In recent years, the issue of income inequality has gained significant attention worldwide, and for good reason. The disparities in wealth and income distribution have far-reaching consequences, creating social, political, and economic challenges for nations across the globe. While many discussions on inequality tend to focus on urban areas and specific industries, it is crucial not to overlook the critical role of rural economies in achieving balanced growth and addressing the broader issue of income inequality.

Rural areas are often characterized by limited access to resources, including education, healthcare, and employment opportunities. This lack of access perpetuates a cycle of poverty and hinders the potential for economic growth and social mobility. To address this issue, policymakers must prioritize empowering rural economies as a means to tackle income inequality.

Investing in education is a fundamental step towards empowering rural communities. Improving the quality of education and expanding access to educational resources in rural areas can provide individuals with the tools they need to secure higher-paying jobs and break free from the cycle of poverty. By bridging the education gap between urban and rural areas, policymakers can unlock the potential of individuals in rural communities and contribute to reducing income inequality.

Additionally, healthcare access is a crucial aspect of empowering rural economies. Limited access to quality healthcare services not only affects the well-being of individuals but also hampers their ability to participate fully in economic activities. By investing in infrastructure, healthcare facilities, and healthcare professionals in rural areas, policymakers can ensure that individuals have equal access to healthcare, regardless of their geographical location. This will not only contribute to better health outcomes but also enable individuals to actively participate in economic activities, thereby reducing income disparities.

Furthermore, fostering entrepreneurship and promoting job creation in rural areas is vital for empowering rural economies. By providing incentives for businesses to establish themselves in rural communities, policymakers can create employment opportunities and stimulate economic growth. This will not only provide individuals with stable income sources but also contribute to the overall development of the region, reducing the income gap between urban and rural areas.

In conclusion, addressing income inequality requires a holistic approach that includes empowering rural economies. By investing in education, healthcare access, and job creation in rural areas, policymakers can contribute to balanced growth and tackle the broader issue of income inequality. It is essential for politicians to recognize the significance of rural economies in the fight against income inequality and implement policies that promote inclusive growth for the benefit of all individuals, regardless of their geographical location or occupation.

Chapter 11: Income Inequality in the Tech Industry

Tech Industry and Wealth Concentration

The tech industry has emerged as a dominant force in our global economy, revolutionizing the way we live, work, and communicate. However, it has also become a major contributor to wealth concentration, exacerbating income inequality across various dimensions.

In terms of world income inequality, the tech industry has deepened the divide between developed and developing countries. While tech giants in developed nations continue to accumulate vast fortunes, the digital divide widens, leaving millions in developing countries without access to the benefits of technological advancements. This inequality is not only economic but also educational, as it hinders the ability of individuals in developing countries to acquire the skills necessary to participate in the digital economy.

Gender income inequality is another area where the tech industry falls short. Despite efforts to promote diversity and inclusion, women remain underrepresented and undervalued in tech-related jobs. This disparity not only affects women's economic well-being but also perpetuates gender inequalities in society as a whole.

Similarly, racial income inequality persists within the tech industry. People from minority backgrounds face barriers to entry and advancement, resulting in a lack of representation at all levels. This not only limits the economic opportunities for individuals from marginalized communities but also perpetuates systemic racism.

Income inequality in education and healthcare access is exacerbated by the tech industry as well. While technology has the potential to improve educational outcomes and increase healthcare accessibility, it often ends up benefiting those who can afford it, leaving disadvantaged individuals further behind. This digital divide not only hampers social mobility but also perpetuates existing inequalities.

Even within the tech industry itself, income inequality is prevalent. The concentration of wealth among a few tech giants and top executives is staggering, while many workers struggle to make ends meet. This disparity is further exacerbated in the gig economy, where workers often lack job security, benefits, and fair wages.

As politicians, it is crucial to address these issues and take action to mitigate the negative consequences of wealth concentration in the tech industry. Policies that promote equal access to technology, enhance diversity and inclusion, and ensure fair wages and working conditions for tech workers can help reduce income inequality across various dimensions.

By recognizing the impact of the tech industry on wealth concentration and income inequality, politicians can play a vital role in shaping a more equitable and inclusive society. It is imperative to leverage the power of technology to bridge the gaps rather than widen them, ensuring that the benefits of technological advancements are accessible to all individuals, regardless of their background or location.

Implications of Tech-Driven Income Inequality

In recent years, technological advancements have significantly impacted various aspects of our lives, including the economy. While these technological innovations have undeniably brought about numerous benefits, they have also exacerbated income inequality on a global scale. As politicians, it is essential to recognize and address the implications of tech-driven income inequality, as it affects a wide range of niches, including world income inequality, gender income inequality, racial income inequality, income inequality in education, income inequality in healthcare access, income inequality in developing and developed countries, income inequality in urban and rural areas, income inequality in the tech industry, and income inequality in the gig economy.

One of the most significant implications of tech-driven income inequality is the exacerbation of global income disparity. While technology has opened up vast opportunities for economic growth and development in certain regions, it has also left others behind, resulting in a significant gap between the world's wealthiest and poorest populations. This disparity not only undermines social cohesion but also hampers the potential for sustainable economic progress.

Moreover, within countries, the tech-driven income inequality has disproportionately affected marginalized communities. Gender income inequality continues to persist, with women facing barriers to accessing high-paying tech jobs and experiencing lower wages compared to their male counterparts in the industry. Similarly, racial income inequality remains a pressing issue, as people from minority communities often face systemic barriers that limit their access to tech-related opportunities.

Education and healthcare, two fundamental pillars of societal well-being, have also been impacted by tech-driven income inequality. The digital divide, which refers to the unequal access to technology and internet connectivity, has hindered educational opportunities for disadvantaged students, perpetuating income inequality in education. Additionally, inadequate access to healthcare services and information due to technological disparities further exacerbate income inequality in healthcare access.

Developing countries, in particular, face unique challenges in addressing tech-driven income inequality. While these nations seek to leverage technology for economic growth, they often lack the necessary infrastructure and resources to fully benefit from technological advancements. This further widens the income gap between developing and developed countries.

Furthermore, income inequality is not limited to urban areas alone. Rural communities often face limited access to tech-related opportunities, resulting in a growing income disparity between urban and rural areas. This disparity hampers the overall development and well-being of rural populations.

In the tech industry and the gig economy, where many jobs are now being created, income inequality is rampant. The concentration of wealth among a few tech giants, coupled with the precarious nature of gig work, contributes to the growing income gap within these sectors.

As politicians, it is imperative to recognize these implications and take proactive measures to address tech-driven income inequality. This may involve policies that promote equal access to education and healthcare, encourage the growth of tech industries in underserved areas, address gender and racial disparities, and foster inclusive economic development. By doing so, we can work towards a more equitable and sustainable future for all.

Encouraging Fairness and Diversity in the Tech Sector

The tech industry plays a pivotal role in shaping our modern world, driving economic growth, and fueling innovation. However, it is also a sector that has been plagued by persistent issues of inequality and lack of diversity. In order to address these challenges and create a more equitable and inclusive tech industry, policymakers must take active steps to encourage fairness and diversity.

One of the key areas where inequality persists in the tech sector is in the distribution of income. The World's Income Inequality is a pressing issue that needs to be tackled. It is essential for politicians to implement policies that promote fair wages and ensure that the benefits of technological advancements are distributed more evenly across society.

Furthermore, gender income inequality remains a significant concern in the tech industry. Women continue to be underrepresented and face unequal pay and limited career advancement opportunities. Policymakers must take proactive measures to encourage gender diversity, such as implementing gender-blind hiring practices and fostering supportive work environments.

Racial income inequality is another aspect that needs urgent attention. People of color are often underrepresented in the tech sector and face systemic barriers that hinder their career progression. Policymakers should work towards creating equal opportunities for individuals from all racial backgrounds, through initiatives such as targeted recruitment and mentorship programs.

Education and healthcare access are also crucial factors that contribute to income inequality. Policymakers must invest in ensuring equal access to quality education and healthcare, particularly in underserved communities. By providing equal opportunities for education and healthcare, we can equip individuals with the skills and resources necessary to thrive in the tech industry.

Income inequality is not limited to developed countries alone; it is equally prevalent in developing countries. Policymakers should focus on creating an enabling environment for tech innovation and entrepreneurship in developing nations, as this can foster economic growth and reduce inequality.

Addressing income inequality in both urban and rural areas is vital. Policymakers must bridge the digital divide by investing in infrastructure and ensuring access to high-speed internet in rural areas. Additionally, efforts should be made to attract tech companies to urban areas and create job opportunities for local communities.

Lastly, addressing income inequality in the tech industry itself is of utmost importance. Policymakers should encourage companies to implement diversity and inclusion initiatives, while also holding them accountable for their progress. This can include setting diversity targets, promoting transparency in hiring practices, and supporting employee resource groups.

In conclusion, the tech sector has the potential to be a driver of economic growth and innovation. However, to fully realize this potential, policymakers must prioritize encouraging fairness and diversity. By addressing income inequality and promoting equal opportunities in education, healthcare, and employment, we can create a more inclusive and equitable tech industry that benefits society as a whole.

Chapter 12: Income Inequality in the Gig Economy

Rise of Gig Work and Income Insecurity

The rise of gig work has become a significant driver of income inequality and income insecurity across various sectors and regions, impacting individuals and communities worldwide. This subchapter explores the implications of gig work on income inequality, shedding light on its effects on various niches such as world's income inequality, gender income inequality, racial income inequality, income inequality in education, income inequality in healthcare access, income inequality in developing and developed countries, income inequality in urban and rural areas, income inequality in the tech industry, and income inequality in the gig economy.

Gig work, characterized by short-term contracts and freelance opportunities, offers flexibility and independence to workers. However, it also exposes them to income volatility and limited access to social protection. This type of work is particularly prevalent in developing countries, where individuals often lack stable employment opportunities and are forced to rely on the gig economy to survive. Consequently, income inequality in these regions is exacerbated, as gig workers struggle to earn a living wage or accumulate wealth.

Furthermore, gender income inequality is perpetuated by gig work. Women are disproportionately represented in low-paying gig jobs and face barriers to advancement within the gig economy. The lack of social protection and benefits further exacerbates gender income inequality. Similarly, racial income inequality is reinforced, as marginalized communities often face discrimination and limited access to high-paying gig work opportunities.

Education and healthcare access also play a crucial role in income inequality. Gig workers often lack access to quality education and healthcare, perpetuating the cycle of poverty and limited economic mobility. This issue is particularly pronounced in both urban and rural areas, where gig work is prevalent, but access to essential services is limited.

The tech industry, which heavily relies on gig workers, showcases a stark income inequality divide. While a select few tech workers earn substantial incomes, the majority of gig workers in the tech industry face low wages and uncertain job prospects. Income inequality within this niche highlights the need for fair labor practices and better protection for gig workers.

In summary, the rise of gig work has intensified income inequality and income insecurity across various niches and regions. Policymakers must address these challenges by implementing comprehensive labor regulations and social protection measures that safeguard the rights and well-being of gig workers. By doing so, we can strive for a more equitable society, where income inequality is reduced, and economic opportunities are accessible to all.

Impacts of Gig Economy on Income Distribution

The gig economy, characterized by temporary and flexible work arrangements, has emerged as a significant force in the labor market. This subchapter aims to explore the impacts of the gig economy on income distribution, shedding light on the various dimensions of inequality that it exacerbates. Addressed to politicians, this analysis seeks to provide a comprehensive overview of the challenges and potential policy responses to mitigate the adverse effects of income inequality in the gig economy.

The gig economy has both positive and negative implications for income distribution. On one hand, it offers increased opportunities for individuals to earn income, especially those who may face barriers to traditional employment. Freelancing and gig work provide a flexible option for individuals, allowing them to balance multiple jobs or pursue other interests. However, this flexibility often comes at the cost of stability and job security, leading to income volatility and an erosion of workers' bargaining power.

One notable impact of the gig economy on income distribution is its contribution to the widening gap between the top earners and the rest of the workforce. While some individuals thrive in the gig economy, earning substantial incomes through high-skilled freelance work or capitalizing on digital platforms, many others experience precarious and low-paying gigs that perpetuate income inequality. This disparity is particularly evident in sectors where gig work is prevalent, such as the tech industry.

Moreover, the gig economy also intersects with other dimensions of inequality, further exacerbating disparities. Gender income inequality, for instance, persists in the gig economy, as women are often concentrated in lower-paying gigs and face barriers to accessing higher-paying opportunities. Racial income inequality is also perpetuated, with minority groups often facing discrimination and limited access to high-paying gigs.

Income inequality in education and healthcare access is another critical aspect influenced by the gig economy. The lack of stable employment and benefits can hinder workers' ability to invest in education or access quality healthcare, limiting social mobility and perpetuating inequality.

These challenges are not limited to specific regions or countries. Income inequality in both developing and developed countries is influenced by the gig economy, albeit in different ways. In urban areas, gig work may provide economic opportunities, but it can also contribute to the rising cost of living and housing inequality. Rural areas, on the other hand, may experience limited access to gig work and suffer from economic marginalization.

To address these impacts, policymakers must consider a range of measures. These may include strengthening labor protections for gig workers, ensuring access to social safety nets, promoting collective bargaining rights, and investing in education and skills development. Additionally, efforts should be made to address discrimination and bias in the allocation of gig work opportunities.

In conclusion, the gig economy has profound effects on income distribution, exacerbating various forms of inequality. To create a fair and inclusive society, politicians must understand these impacts and develop policies that address the challenges faced by gig workers while promoting income equality across all dimensions of society.

Policies for Ensuring Fairness in the Gig Economy

The gig economy, characterized by short-term contracts and freelance work, has experienced rapid growth in recent years. While it offers flexibility and opportunities for individuals to earn income, it also presents challenges in terms of fairness and income inequality. In this subchapter, we will explore policies that can be implemented to ensure fairness in the gig economy, addressing various aspects such as income inequality, gender, race, education, healthcare access, and regional disparities.

One key policy that can promote fairness in the gig economy is the establishment of a minimum wage for gig workers. Currently, many gig workers struggle to earn a living wage due to the unpredictable nature of gig work and the lack of bargaining power. Implementing a minimum wage would provide a safety net and protect workers from exploitation, ensuring a baseline level of income for all gig workers.

Moreover, it is crucial to address gender income inequality in the gig economy. Women often face lower pay and limited opportunities compared to their male counterparts. To combat this, policies should focus on promoting equal pay for equal work, ensuring that women have access to the same opportunities and are not discriminated against based on gender. Additionally, providing affordable childcare options and flexible work arrangements can help women balance their caregiving responsibilities with gig work.

Similarly, racial income inequality is a pressing issue in the gig economy. Minorities often face barriers to entry and experience discrimination in accessing gig work. Policies should aim to eliminate discriminatory practices and promote diversity and inclusion in the gig economy. Encouraging partnerships between gig platforms and community organizations can help connect marginalized communities with gig work opportunities.

Furthermore, addressing income inequality in education and healthcare access is crucial to ensuring fairness in the gig economy. Policies should focus on providing affordable and accessible education and healthcare services to gig workers. This can include subsidized training programs and affordable healthcare plans tailored to the needs of gig workers.

Lastly, regional disparities in income inequality must be addressed. In both urban and rural areas, gig workers may face different challenges and opportunities. Policies should be tailored to the specific needs of each region, providing support and resources to bridge the income gap between urban and rural gig workers.

In conclusion, the gig economy presents both opportunities and challenges in terms of fairness and income inequality. Implementing policies such as establishing a minimum wage, addressing gender and racial disparities, improving education and healthcare access, and addressing regional disparities can help ensure fairness and reduce income inequality in the gig economy. As policymakers, it is crucial to recognize the importance of these policies and take action to create a more equitable gig economy for all.

Chapter 13: Conclusion: A Call to Action for Politicians

The Role of Politics in Tackling Income Inequality

Income inequality is a pressing issue that affects various aspects of society, including the world's income distribution, gender, race, education, healthcare access, and even specific industries such as the tech sector and gig economy. In addressing these disparities, politics plays a crucial role in implementing policies and driving change.

Politicians, as representatives of the people, are uniquely positioned to address income inequality on a global scale. The world's income inequality has reached alarming levels, with the richest 1% owning more wealth than the rest of the world combined. To combat this, politicians must prioritize policies that promote fair taxation, establish progressive income redistribution mechanisms, and foster economic growth that benefits all.

Gender income inequality remains a persistent issue, where women continue to face wage gaps and limited opportunities for advancement. Policymakers must enforce equal pay legislation, promote gender parity in leadership positions, and provide affordable childcare options to remove barriers that hinder women's economic progress.

Similarly, racial income inequality requires targeted policies that address systemic discrimination and create inclusive economic opportunities. Politicians should advocate for equal access to quality education and job training programs, as well as implement affirmative action policies to level the playing field for marginalized communities.

Income inequality in education and healthcare access further perpetuates social and economic disparities. To tackle these issues, politicians must invest in high-quality public education, expand access to affordable healthcare, and provide comprehensive social services to ensure that no one is left behind.

Developing countries often face extreme income disparities due to limited resources and unequal distribution of wealth. Politicians must prioritize poverty reduction strategies, invest in infrastructure development, and promote sustainable economic growth to uplift these nations.

In developed countries, income inequality persists despite high levels of overall wealth. Policymakers should aim to reduce the wealth gap by implementing progressive tax systems, strengthening social safety nets, and addressing the root causes of inequality, such as the concentration of power and wealth in the hands of a few.

The urban-rural divide is another aspect of income inequality that politicians must address. By investing in rural infrastructure, promoting agricultural modernization, and creating economic opportunities in rural areas, politicians can bridge the gap and ensure that all citizens have access to quality jobs and services.

The tech industry and gig economy have contributed to income disparities as well, with a small group reaping the benefits of digitalization while many struggle to make ends meet. Policymakers must regulate these sectors, promote workers' rights, and provide support for those affected by automation and job displacement.

In conclusion, politics plays a vital role in tackling income inequality across various niches. By implementing comprehensive and targeted policies, politicians can create a more equitable society, bridging the gaps in income distribution and ensuring that no one is left behind. The Economics of Inequality: A Call to Action for Politicians serves as a guide for policymakers to understand the importance of their role and take concrete steps towards a fairer future.

Policy Recommendations to Reduce Income Inequality

Addressing income inequality is a pressing issue that requires immediate attention from policymakers around the world. As politicians, you have the power to implement policies that can help alleviate this problem and create a more equitable society. This subchapter provides a comprehensive set of policy recommendations to tackle income inequality across various domains.

1. World's Income Inequality: Encourage international cooperation and fair trade policies to ensure developing countries have a fair chance to compete in global markets. Promote initiatives that support economic development in low-income countries, such as foreign aid and debt relief.

2. Gender Income Inequality: Implement policies that promote gender pay equity, such as pay transparency and equal pay legislation. Support initiatives that provide affordable childcare, parental leave, and flexible work arrangements to help women balance work and family responsibilities.

3. Racial Income Inequality: Develop targeted policies to address systemic discrimination and promote equal opportunities for marginalized communities. Increase access to quality education, job training, and affordable housing in disadvantaged areas.

4. Income Inequality in Education: Invest in high-quality public education, particularly in low-income areas, to ensure equal access to educational opportunities. Implement policies that reduce the cost of higher education and provide support for students from disadvantaged backgrounds.

5. Income Inequality in Healthcare Access: Expand access to affordable healthcare through universal healthcare systems or reforms that increase coverage and reduce out-of-pocket expenses. Invest in preventative care and address the social determinants of health to reduce disparities.

6. Income Inequality in Developing Countries: Promote inclusive economic growth by investing in infrastructure, healthcare, and education. Encourage entrepreneurship and job creation to stimulate economic opportunities in rural and urban areas alike.

7. Income Inequality in Developed Countries: Implement progressive taxation policies to redistribute wealth and reduce income disparities. Increase public investment in social safety nets, including healthcare, education, and unemployment benefits.

8. Income Inequality in Urban Areas: Develop affordable housing programs and initiatives that promote community development in urban areas. Invest in public transportation and infrastructure to improve access to job opportunities.

9. Income Inequality in Rural Areas: Support rural development through investment in agriculture, infrastructure, and job creation. Improve access to education, healthcare, and technology in rural communities.

10. Income Inequality in the Tech Industry: Encourage diversity and inclusion in the tech sector through targeted recruitment and retention policies. Invest in digital literacy programs to bridge the digital divide and provide equal opportunities for all.

11. Income Inequality in the Gig Economy: Establish regulations that protect workers' rights and ensure fair wages and benefits for gig economy workers. Develop social safety nets tailored to the needs of gig workers, such as portable benefits and access to healthcare.

By implementing these policy recommendations, you can make significant strides in reducing income inequality within your respective areas of influence. Remember, addressing income inequality is not only a moral imperative but also an economic necessity for a more prosperous and just society.

Mobilizing Political Will for a More Equitable Future

In the face of growing income inequality across the globe, the need for political action has become more urgent than ever before. As politicians, you have the power to shape policies and create a more equitable future for all. This subchapter aims to inspire and guide you in mobilizing political will to address various dimensions of income inequality that exist in our world today.

First and foremost, it is crucial to recognize the multifaceted nature of income inequality. From the world's income inequality to gender, racial, and regional disparities, each dimension requires targeted efforts and tailored solutions. By understanding the unique challenges faced by different groups, you can develop policies that address their specific needs.

Addressing income inequality in education and healthcare access is vital for building a fairer society. By investing in quality education for all, regardless of socio-economic background, you can empower individuals to overcome the barriers that perpetuate inequality. Similarly, ensuring equal access to affordable healthcare services will not only improve health outcomes but also contribute to reducing economic disparities.

While income inequality is often associated with developing countries, it is important to acknowledge that it exists in developed nations as well. By implementing progressive tax systems, increasing the minimum wage, and promoting inclusive economic policies, you can mitigate the growing income gap within your own countries.

Furthermore, income inequality is not limited to urban areas. Rural communities also face unique challenges, such as limited access to quality education, healthcare, and job opportunities. By investing in rural infrastructure, promoting entrepreneurship, and expanding social safety nets, you can uplift these communities and create a more balanced society.

Income inequality in specific industries, such as the tech sector and the gig economy, also demands attention. As politicians, you can push for fair labor practices, ensure equal pay for equal work, and encourage diversity and inclusion in these sectors.

To mobilize political will effectively, collaboration is key. Engage with academics, economists, civil society organizations, and grassroots movements to understand the root causes of income inequality and develop evidence-based policies. Foster dialogue and inclusivity, actively seeking input from individuals and communities affected by income disparities.

In conclusion, tackling income inequality requires a comprehensive and concerted effort from politicians across the globe. By recognizing the diverse dimensions of inequality and tailoring policies accordingly, you can create a more equitable future for all. Let us come together, mobilize political will, and take decisive action to build a fairer and more just society.